You are in a

Wonderful World

Mindfulness - Guide to Awakening

Personal Growth, Positive Thinking
Self-Esteem, Continuous Improvement

Aurora Gadhatta

YOU ARE IN A WONDERFUL WORLD

DEDICATION

To all those people who are constantly on the move, towards new horizons, in search of a "buried port", hidden inside, to discover new side of themselves, with the hope that they will find the right "passage" that leads to Life.

YOU ARE IN A WONDERFUL WORLD

TABLE OF CONTENTS

Introduction

Conclusion

Introduction

It is no secret that we are living in a society that is fast-paced, stressed out, and often stretched far too thin. Every day, people are finding themselves growing more frustrated, overwhelmed, and distressed by the lives that they are living. For many, the idea of a solution seems hard-pressed or nearly impossible. "That's just the way it is," they say, as they go about their lives, continually building on their already-enormous levels of stress and driving themselves to the ground day after day. For many, the idea of a life that could be anything other than borderline miserable seems like a far-off dream that will probably never come true.

In our society, people live for the weekends. They do the things that they "have to do," and they burn themselves out time and again, never fully allowing themselves to recover and recuperate in between. For many, the symptoms of stress build on each other until the individual eventually becomes so ill from the stress they have placed on their body that they can no longer participate in normal day-to-day activities. Our society's standard way of approaching life is dysfunctional, at best.

These days, everyone seems to be searching for the best answer as to how they can change their approach and begin to enjoy life in a more wholesome, enjoyable, and powerful manner. People want to know how they can step away from the daily grind and begin to feel at peace and empowered in their lives, rather than at the mercy of their to-do list and their busy schedules. They are searching for answers, and many are finding solutions. Like you, right now, reading this book is a way to find a solution.

One of the best solutions that we can turn to when it comes to healing ourselves from the stressors of everyday life in modern society is mindfulness. Mindfulness allows us to awaken to the world around us, recalling what truly matters and setting our priorities straight when it comes to approaching life on a daily basis. When we begin to use mindfulness daily, it teaches us to slow down, look within, and take the necessary efforts to cultivate happiness, peace, and joy within ourselves. Through mindfulness, we essentially turn ourselves into the change maker of our own lives, directly giving ourselves the power to change the narrative of the lives we are living so that we can tell a story that better suits the very fibers of who we are and who we wish to be.

Over the next nine chapters, we are going to spend time together, learning, growing, and healing. You might find yourself laughing at times, crying at others, or simply going "oh" as you discover new pieces of information that can help you change the entire outlook of your life, forever.

If you are here feeling skeptical about the power of mindfulness, trust me when I say that you are not alone. Thousands of people just like you have found themselves here before, searching for an answer and questioning whether or not they have found one that is good enough for their needs. When they discover mindfulness, many think it is too good to be true. They are worried that if they put all of their hope into one answer, they might be painfully let down and that they could find themselves feeling worse than they did when they started on this journey. I want to tell you that it's not too good to be true. It is a well-known fact in psychology that mindfulness helps us improve our ability to manage stress, approach life in a more enjoyable way, and live better lives overall.

The key is to understand that mindfulness takes time to develop and that you have to put the necessary effort to achieve a state of mindful living. If you truly want to see your life transform, you are going to have to flex your mindfulness like a muscle and tap into it again and again until it becomes your natural, automatic response to the life that is happening all around you. Through this consistent practice, you will find relief from the stressors and struggles of everyday life.

If you are ready to begin putting in the effort to make the transformation in your own life, it is time for us to begin! Please, as you approach this journey, be gentle with yourself. Be patient with the results that are coming, and trust that your continued efforts are going to provide you with wonderful, magical results as you go. Be honest with yourself; take it at your own pace. Most of all, have fun learning about this new process that is going to change your life as you know it.

Let's begin.

Chapter 1

How Mindfulness

Supports Personal Growth

Before you can really tap into using mindfulness as a tool to help you grow, it is important to know *how* it helps you. In my experience, many people struggle to gain support or relief from something if they cannot understand why or how it is meant to be helping them in the first place. Spending some time learning about this part of your mindful journey is going to help you appeal to the logical part of your brain that likes to answer the questions "why?" and "how?" Once you have appealed to this part of your brain, you will be able to dig deeper into the experience of mindfulness itself,

1

allowing you to gain everything that it has to offer.

As you read through this chapter, take the time to understand why mindfulness is going to be so powerful for you. I encourage you to read through this chapter with an open mind so that any skepticism or worries that you might be facing right now can be reasonably answered and addressed, allowing you to approach the rest of the journey with the open-mindedness that is required for you to succeed.

What Is Mindfulness?

Mindfulness has become somewhat of a buzz word in the past decade or so, and with good reason. This particular way of life is one that has the power to help alleviate an entire society of the stresses and woes that we have found ourselves facing each day in our lives. That being said, it is important to remember that mindfulness is a real, valid, and helpful tool that can support you in having a higher quality of life. Mindfulness is not meant to be a trend that you engage with for a few weeks, see some placebo effects from, and then give up on. Unlike other fads that rise and fall in our society, mindfulness is a real, useful tool that can help you change your life.

Beyond that, mindfulness is not something that is challenging to achieve. In fact, your brain already engages in mindfulness every single day. However, the chances are you have not yet taught yourself to use mindfulness in a way that it can serve you, so instead, it is working against you. In other words, rather than becoming mindful, which can actually support you in leading high quality of life, you may be mindfully aware of the things that are preventing you from having a good life. So, you end up fixating on the things that are not capable of helping you live your best life, thus causing you to feel worse at the end of every single day.

Mindfulness naturally happens every single time you notice the color, shape, or appearance of something. When you notice where a certain sound is coming from or what is causing a certain sensation in your body, you are engaging with mindfulness. Each time you pay attention to the taste of your food or the smell around you, you are being mindful. So, as you can see, you are already amazing at being mindful.

Mindfulness, at its core, is a behavior that we engage in when we become *mindful of something.* In other words, any time you become conscious or aware of something, you are giving it your full attention. This means that you are mindful of it. This is an extremely simple behavior to engage in since your brain is already doing it.Now, you just need to teach your brain how to master it in a specific way so that you can begin leading high quality of life.

What Does Mindfulness Do?

When we engage in a state of mindfulness, we purposefully relax our brain and allow it to focus on just one thing at a time. During this time, our goal is not to judge or react to something, but instead to become aware of what it is. Creating this awareness helps us begin to have a more relaxing, peaceful acceptance of our reality, which has been shown to provide us with positive outcomes in terms of how it nurtures us both psychologically and physically.

The psychological and physical benefits that we gain from mindfulness are not just a placebo effect, either. Mindfulness actually creates real, identifiable changes in the brain that result in a tangible, physical foundation for these psychological and physical changes to occur. In 2014, there was a study done where researchers took images of people's brains both before and after they engaged in a deep mindfulness session. They studied people who were new to mindfulness, as well as those who had been engaging in mindfulness meditation sessions for a long period. What they found was that the people who engaged in mindfulness, both as beginners and intermediate practitioners, had a greater sense of self-awareness around their thoughts and emotions. They also had more awareness of their body, particularly around their sensory experiences through their sensory cortices and insula. Their hippocampus, which was responsible for memory, was also more active and functional, so was their ability to practice self-regulation and emotional regulation. Finally, those who regularly engaged in mindfulness also had better communication between parts of their brains, which means that their bodies functioned better overall.

Physically, mindfulness does plenty as well. The people involved in the study were also found to have lower reactivity to stress, including lowered blood pressure and lowered heart and respiratory rates. These individuals engaging in mindfulness were also more likely to activate their parasympathetic nervous system, which is responsible for "rest and digest" mode, rather than their sympathetic nervous system which is responsible for "flight or fight" mode. This activation directly contributes to many physical changes in the body, including lowered cortisol levels, lowered C-reactive proteins, and lowered interleukin 6. These characteristics help individuals by lowering their risk of blood pressure disorders, heart irregularities, chronic fatigue, insomnia, digestive disorders, reduced fertility, mental health issues, and even diabetes.

This study was not the only study that proved these findings. Hundreds of studies have been done over the past two decades, and they have consistently proven the same findings when it comes to mindfulness. People who engage in mindfulness actually change physically that, over time, the entire trajectory of their liveschanges as well.

How Will Mindfulness
Support Personal Growth?

Mindfulness is the practice of turning your focus toward something intentionally. Often, a core element of mindfulness practices involves observing your own perception of the experiences that you are having in your life. For example, a popular mindfulness experience is to eat a raisin slowly so that you can become mindfully aware of what the experience of eating a raisin feels like for you. The result is that you become more aware of yourself, including your unique way of experiencing the world around you.

This increased self-awareness and ability to understand how you experience the world around you helps you identify what your patterns are, as well as your strengths and weaknesses and how various experiences make you feel. Through this, you can identify opportunities for you to engage in self-growth or personal development by identifying areas in your life where you can improve your response to what is happening around you. For example, let's say that you find yourself getting extremely stressed out about work every single day to the point where it is causing you to feel overwhelmed and frustrated about the general topic of work. You know that you cannot afford to quit your job, so you must stay, leaving you feeling as though there is no viable solution for the way you are feeling on a day to day basis. Of course, this is not entirely true. By engaging in mindfulness, you can begin to become aware of what parts of your career are leading to this enormous level of stress; then you can mindfully choose a new approach that will support you to feel less stressed around the topic of work. Perhaps your new approach includes physically approaching situations in a different way, such as improving your organization skills or your punctuality skills. Or maybe, your new approach includes you mentally approaching situations in a new way by perceiving them differently, either by putting less pressure on them or by offering yourself the opportunity to see a way that they could be more manageable.

Arguably, personal growth cannot truly happen without mindfulness because, without it, we would have no idea what needs focus in terms of our personal growth efforts. Self-awareness caused by mindfulness is the first step to an effective personal development or personal growth strategy, which means that developing your mindfulness will only further improve your personal growth efforts.

How Long Do I Have to Be Mindful?

Many people confuse mindfulness with meditation, which is why questions like this tend to be common for people who are just beginning to embark on their mindfulness journey. As we will discuss in Chapter 4, there are some fundamental differences between mindfulness and meditation, including what they are and how they work. While they do work together to create a full experience, they are not the same thing.

This means that mindfulness itself is something that you actually want to experience as often as you possibly can. While it may not be feasible to think that a person could be mindful every minute of every day, it is reasonable to think that we can stop and have frequent mindfulness checks that will allow us to continue to behave in a mindful way.

It might sound overwhelming or unreasonable to try to live your life mindfully as often as you possibly can, especially if you are someone who does not currently live in a state of mindful awareness on a regular basis. Trust that the process of cultivating your mindfulness will happen at the right pace for you, and as it begins to grow and integrate into more of your day to day life, it will come naturally to you. The idea of being mindful or mindfully questioning your life experiences every time something significant happens to you will become more reasonable, and you will do it more consistently.

Each time you engage in mindfulness, your brain changes, as you now know. This means that your brain will naturally begin to respond to things in your life more mindfully, even when you are not actively thinking about it. It seems like a contradiction, especially because mindful awareness means that we need to be aware of our mindfulness, but it will become somewhat of a habit for you. You will find yourself naturally engaging in a mindful state of *awareness* every single time that it is needed, allowing you to tap into it as often as possible. This will allow you to live your best quality of life and have your best experiences going forward.

Chapter 2

Transforming Your Thinking Patterns

The very first step in becoming more mindfully aware and awakening yourself through the power of mindfulness is to transform your thinking patterns. Your thinking patterns are responsible for virtually everything in your entire life, as they determine the part of your life that you are going to become aware of. Your thought processes help you identify what you think is important in your environment, cultivate an opinion around what it is, and then determine what reaction or response you are going to have to that stimuli.

Learning how to become mindfully aware of your thoughts allows you to transform your thinking patterns, which will lay the entire foundation for you to begin experiencing a more mindful life. This is where your mindful approach to personal growth will come in. It is where you will find yourself immediately making changes in the way that you perceive and experience life, and it is where you will begin to witness the unfolding of your personal awakening.

Transforming your thinking patterns will take effort, self-awareness, and willingness to commit to your mindfulness journey every single day. Understand that transforming your thinking patterns is a unique experience for everyone, so some people might find it to be frustrating or overwhelming, and others might find it to be rather simple. How the experience will feel for you depends entirely on your patterns and experiences in life itself. There is no right or wrong length of time or amount of effort that it would take to create your transformation in the way that you think. Likewise, there is no reason to think that any amount of time or effort involved is either good or bad. Instead, they are simply personal experiences that you are enjoying in your life as you work toward having a better experience overall.

In this chapter, we are going to cover the steps that it typically takes to help you mindfully change your mind so that you can begin engaging in healthier thinking patterns. Understand that this is a guide, so you might find yourself requiring alterations to the approach that you must take for your personal change. Again, there is no right or wrong, bad or good approach to creating these transformations. Take this guideline, enforce it in your own life, and then allow yourself to begin identifying where it is working and where you can adapt it to help give you the best results. Through this approach, you will learn massively about yourself, the way that you experience the world around you, and the way that you can successfully work with yourself to have the best possible life experience.

The Process of Habitual Thinking

Our thoughts, like most things in our lives, form as more of a habitual experience than anything else. In its natural state, our brain likes to make everything as efficient as possible so that it consumes as little energy as possible. This is intended to support our survival, as the less energy our brain consumes, the more energy can be used in other areas of our bodies, such as digesting food or simply going through the physical motions of day to day life. It also reserves a fair amount of energy for those moments where we need a sudden burst in energy, such as when our fight or flight response needs to kick in to help us get across the street faster or make clearer and quicker decisions during an important meeting.

Your brain's habitual thoughts are determined based on your previous experiences and what has worked for you in the past. Your brain creates these thoughts by identifying a trigger that seems to stimulate a similar thought response every single time. For example, let's say that you find unicorns to be particularly interesting, and you find joy every time you see a unicorn picture printed on things. Every time you see a unicorn t-shirt, your brain is going to recall the fascination that you had with the image and respond with a thought along the lines of "hey, that's cool. I like that." Eventually, you are not even going to notice the fascination of your thoughts anymore. Instead, you will just have an immediate response of "hey, that's cool. I like that." This way, your brain does not have to go through the entire decision-making process of deciding whether or not you actually like the shirt again, which can require you to identify and process a large amount of information. Instead, it skips the entire decision-making process and jumps straight to the memory of you determining that you liked unicorn images in the first place.

This does not just happen for cool things, as you know. This response process happens to everything in your life, regardless of what it is or what response it is stimulating. This means, in many cases, your responses of joy, anger, frustration, irritation, happiness, excitement, fear, sadness, and other responses are often stimulated as more of a habit than an actual mindful experience. This does not mean that you do not experience new or mindful emotions or thoughts at any point in your life, but it does mean that many of the emotions and thoughts that you are going to experience in your life will be habitual.

Also, in many cases, your new thoughts are going to be determined by an alternative habit that you have when it comes to how you think about things in your life. For example, let's say that you tend to have a pessimistic outlook, and you find that you regularly complain about things and that you find yourself often identifying the worst in new situations that you are facing. In this case, if you were to face a new situation in your life that you had never experienced before, complete with new thoughts and emotions, you would still respond to that situation in a habitual way. That is, you would look for the worst in the situation and would likely find something to complain about right away. In this case, while the content of your thoughts and emotions were not habitual, the way that they were formulated was.

Identifying your thinking habits is key to helping you

transition away from habitual thinking processes to mindful ones. This way, you can identify what your natural response or pattern would be, and you can then choose a new response to the pattern that will serve you better in the long run. The mindfulness part of the experience comes in. By helping you identify when the unwanted or unhelpful habits were triggered, as well as understand how you can implement and integrate the new habit that is also beneficial and more desirable, you transition to mindfulness.

A great way to begin identifying your habits so that you can begin to make changes is to keep a thought journal. Many people who are engaging in a mindful journey use a thought journal as a way to track the nature of their thoughts, the habitual thoughts that they are experiencing, and the way that they tend to respond to new information. This way, they can quickly discover what their thought patterns and habits are on a regular basis, helping them to identify a new and more plausible way forward. Keeping a thought journal yourself will help you identify where your thoughts are supporting you and where they are causing you to struggle so that when you are ready to begin mindfully changing your thoughts, you know what it is that you want to change in the first place.

Setting the Intention and Being Patient

After you have identified where your thoughts are not serving you, it is up to you to decide how you want to adapt your thinking behaviors so that you can have a healthier thought pattern. In other words, you need to decide how you want to change the nature of your thoughts and how you want your changed mind to look like. This is not only going to give you a clearer goal on how you want to approach your new thinking patterns, but it also gives you a clear set of guidelines on how you should adjust your thoughts as you move forward. This way, each time you have a negative and unhelpful thought, you know what to do in order to modify it to become a positive thought that is more beneficial to your well-being.

Setting the intention of the type of new thought processes you want to have starts by understanding how you want to feel and how your thoughts contribute

22

to your feelings. On a very basic level, thoughts trigger emotions by helping us identify important parts of our environment or experiences that can stimulate an emotional response. For example, if you walk into a home and think, "wow, this is comfortable," you are likely to begin feeling at ease and calm in your experience. However, if you walk into a home and think, "wow, this is overwhelming and messy. I feel unsafe," you are likely going to begin feeling uncomfortable and possibly anxious around the situation that you are in.

The best way to set the intention as to how you want your new thoughts to look like is to determine what you want to feel. Since your thoughts stimulate certain emotions, choosing the emotions that you want to feel as a result of your new thinking process can help you identify the guideline for how you will proceed. In the long run, taking this approach saves you energy, which means that you are appealing to the part of your brain that wants to make everything as efficient as it possibly can. This saving of energy occurs when you realize that in each new situations, you do not have to pick a brand new way of thinking. Instead, you just need to consider how you can align your thoughts to produce the emotions that you desire to feel.

After you have determined how you want to feel in each situation, the thinking part will come into alignment naturally. That being said, it has to *come into* alignment. It will not immediately be aligned in the sense that every time you have a new thought, going forward, it becomes perfectly aligned with your brand new way of thinking. You will find that it takes several attempts for you to get it into alignment and begin to think along your new desired way of thinking naturally and habitually. As you continue to focus on your goal and work toward it, you will discover that the alignment happens naturally and, eventually, it is completely in place.

To help yourself forward with these intentions, you *must* practice patience. If you are not patient with yourself, you may reinforce old, unhealthy thinking habits or even create new ones because you teach yourself to be unkind, impatient, and forceful with your changes. In the end, this will not help you change anything; it will only lead you to feel more frustrated. The biggest key to cultivating more patience in your transformation experience is to create more trust in yourself and the process. Trust that each time you begin to engage in mindfulness, you are going to find yourself naturally engaging in it easier the next time around and commit to experiencing changes in your mindfulness as much as you can reasonably handle every single time. It will continue to improve as you move forward.

Challenging Your Automatic Process

When it comes to the process of actually transforming your thoughts, you are going to need to have a strategy in place. This strategy is going to help you transform your thoughts the moment you begin to have unwanted or unhelpful thoughts, allowing you to conduct the transformation process effectively. Without a strategy in place for you to enact anytime you have these unhelpful thoughts, it will be difficult for you to create change because you will find yourself consistently engaging in these negative thoughts despite knowing that you want to approach them differently. Although you may be able to become aware of them and make subtle changes, making any real, lasting change will be challenging because you may not be equipped with the right tools to make changes that will stick in the long run.

The first thing that needs to be changed whenever you find yourself mindfully becoming aware of a thought pattern that you need to modify is changing the way that you perceive each thought. Remember that just because you think something, it does not mean that it is the absolute truth or that there are no other

26

thoughts, opinions, or judgments that you can hold about the said topic. A great way to begin the mindful process is to challenge every single thought that you have, especially when you become aware of the fact that they are not helpful thoughts for your mental health.

Challenging your thoughts gives you the opportunity to determine whether or not you truly believe in what you are presently thinking, and if that thought is actually true. When you ask the two most important questions to challenge your thoughts, you set yourself to decide if you want to continue thinking in the way that you have been. If you decide that you do not, then you can begin to engage in your transformation to choose a better approach to your thought patterns.

The first question you need to ask is: "do I genuinely believe in this?" If you have a thought and you do genuinely believe in it or the angle that it has taken on, this does not mean that it is absolutely true. This just means that you feel it is true based on the current information that is available to you. If you have a thought, and you do not genuinely believe in what it is

27

about, then you know that there is room for you to educate yourself on an alternative way of thinking. You can then begin looking into those alternative ways and finding a different way of thinking that you can genuinely believe in. This way, you are not staying committed to a thought that you do not ultimately believe in.

The next question you need to ask yourself is, "do I know this to be true?" For this question, you want to think about knowledge outside of yourself. In other words, do you have fact-based, scientific-based, or other strong evidence that suggests that your thoughts are, in fact, true? If you do not know it to be true, you know that you may need to do more research to identify whether or not you are actually correct. If you do know for a fact that what you are thinking is true, then you know that you have a strong thought that can support you in certain situations.

Let's look at two examples where these questions are used—one where they support the original thought process and one where they help the individual transform what they are thinking. This way, as you begin to engage in using these two strategies, you can feel confident that you are using them effectively.

For the first scenario, let's say that you have a thought that drunk driving is bad. This thought is based on what you personally believe in, but it is also based on the fact that you have seen an overwhelming amount of evidence that suggests that people who drive when intoxicated present high risk to other people on the road. In this case, if you ask, "do I believe in this?" and you say yes, and then you ask, "do I ultimately know this to be true?" and you say yes, then you know that the thought that you have about drunk driving is aligned and factual. In this case, no transformation is needed because the way you think about alcohol and driving is already true, and it serves you in what you believe in and what you think.

For the second scenario, let's say that you have a

thought that you are a bad friend because you refused to let your friend drive home after having a few drinks at your house despite knowing that they needed to be home first thing in the morning for an important appointment. Perhaps that friend got angry with you and said rude things to you, making you feel bad about your decision. If you begin to think, "I am a bad friend because of this," you can then ask yourself, "do I genuinely believe in this?" and your answer will likely be, "no." Then, you can ask yourself, "do I know that it is ultimately true?" and your answer will likely be, "no" again. Even though you may feel bad for your friend for not being where they need to be on time, you would realize that you were, in fact, a good friend based on your own standards because you were looking out for the safety of your friend.

Although these two scenarios may seem obvious, there are many less obvious situations you will encounter in your life where it feels a little more challenging to identify whether or not you genuinely believe in your thoughts or know them to be true. For these scenarios, you may have to put more work into identifying whether or not you believe in them or if they are true. This may seem like somewhat of a hassle, but in the long run, it will help you immensely in your mindful thinking because you will feel confident in your thoughts. It will also help prevent you from holding onto thoughts that are ultimately untrue, such as thoughts like, "I am a bad person" or "every time something goes good in my life, something comes along to ruin it." This way, you can begin to move away from those negative thoughts that were previously causing you to feel miserable and stressed out on a regular basis.

Acknowledging Unhelpful Thoughts

As you begin to challenge your thoughts, you are going to notice that you have many unhelpful and discouraging thoughts. As humans, we have something in our psyche that is known as "negativity bias." Negative bias means that we naturally lean toward having more pessimistic thoughts because these thoughts are believed to support our survival. In other words, we are more likely to look for the dangers in any situation, whether they are physical, emotional, or mental so that we can prevent ourselves from being affected by those dangers. As we come to learn over time, many of these dangers do exist but are highly unlikely, which means that all the time we invest in worrying about them is ultimately wasted. Since they never come to fruition, we put ourselves on edge, and we grow worried about them for no reason, causing us to experience stress and overwhelming emotions for nothing.

When you challenge your thoughts, you will discover that all your thoughts that are rooted in negativity bias are often unhelpful. Not only do they cause you to spend time overly worried about unlikely dangers, but they also prevent you from having the capacity to focus on positive things that allow you to have a more positive experience.

The best way to overcome negativity bias mindfully is to allow yourself to become aware of your negative or unhelpful thoughts. You can do this by being honest about having them, as well as actions like denying, minimizing, or justifying these thoughts. These actions are only going to lead you to face more challenges. Being honest about the fact that you have a tendency to think negative thoughts will allow you to search for ways to overcome those negative thoughts and help you move forward.

When you do identify an unhelpful or negative thought, it is a good idea to grab your thought journal and write about it. Write down what the thought is, why you think that you have this thought, and what you think this thought serves you. Gather as much information around these unhelpful or negative thoughts as you can, including the other times that you recall having these thoughts, what may have caused the original thought, and whether or not you think this thought is supporting you. The more information you can gather about these thoughts, the easier it is going to be for you to determine what needs to be done in order for you to transform these thoughts.

Practicing the Art of Non-Judgment

After you have identified what your thoughts are and where they come from, you need to assess them and all of the information relating to them in a non-judgmental way. This means that you are going to develop an understanding of what they are and why they exist without creating an emotional involvement or attachment as to why it is happening. Practicing the art of non-judgment with your thoughts is one of the most compassionate ways where you can develop a stronger sense of understanding around yourself and who you are on a deeper level. This allows you to create a stronger awareness of what has influenced you in the past, why you have certain thought patterns, and how they are affecting and implicating you at present.

Think of this part as if you are looking through the eyes of a detective. Here, you are building a case that identifies what your thoughts are and why they happen. This creates a sort of trail that helps you get to the root cause of unhelpful thoughts while also understanding how they are affecting you in their total capacity in your current life. For example, maybe you have an unhelpful thought that says, "I can never do anything right." When you put your non-judgmental detective hat on, you might discover that this is ultimately untrue and that you do many things right. Then, you can begin to identify where this thought comes from and what it creates in your life. Maybe after some contemplation, you realize that growing up, you had a critical parent who was constantly punishing you for never getting anything right, even though you were just making typical childhood mistakes. Now, in your adulthood, perhaps this very thought pattern creates anxiety within you and makes you feel too scared to try new things for fear of not getting it right and being punished when the results are not perfect. With this complete understanding of where this thought pattern comes from, you can now take the appropriate action to heal and then transform this thought in a mindful and complete manner.

Accepting and Letting Be

Nearly every thought can be healed through acceptance, letting be, and allowing things to be. When it comes to transforming your thoughts, there are going to be many layers that need to take place in order for you to heal the negative thought pattern completely. You are going to need to become accepting of yourself and the root cause of the thought. You also need to be accepting anyone else involved in your thought pattern and the consequences that you have faced as a result of this thought. You also need to accept the fact that it is going to take time for changes to happen and that there will be uncomfortable experiences or emotions you face while you undertake the transformation process.

When it comes to creating this level of acceptance, the best thing you can do is affirm your acceptance to yourself and the situation that you are facing. As often as you can, say, "I accept that this is how it has been, and I accept that I can now change the way it is going to be going forward." For example, let's expand on the thought of "I can never do anything right." For this one, you would want to accept yourself for the thoughts and feelings that you felt when you were told that you were not good enough by your critical parent. You would also want to accept your parent and the experience that you two shared in any way that you could. This may not mean accepting their *behavior*, but it could mean that you accept it happened and that it implicated your past and present. Then, you would need to accept that you are having this thought and accept the implications that it has had on your life, including any consequences that you have faced as a result of this thought pattern. Next, you would need to accept that changing this thought is going to take effort and that you are going to have to put in a significant amount of work to begin having newer, healthier thoughts in your life. Once you have completely accepted the situation, you will have mindfully achieved the state of compassion and understanding that you need to be patient with yourself and to support yourself moving forward.

The acceptance phase of any change can be time-consuming, as there is a lot that needs to be accepted.

However, it is crucial to put the energy into being accepting of the experiences you have had and the way that they have impacted your thought process, as this will help you have a deeper understanding of yourself and why you think and feel the way you do. This way, as you begin to make your transformations by identifying, choosing, and committing to new thoughts, you learn to be patient and accepting of yourself along the way.

Finding a Harmonious Way of Thinking

After you have become accepting of yourself and the thought-based experiences that you have been having, you are ready to begin identifying a new solution for how you can think going forward. This is where you can take your intentions and begin to identify mindfully a strategy for how you want to proceed with your thoughts. This way, you can identify thoughts that are going to support you to feel more of the way that you want to feel.

Finding a harmonious way of thinking is where you get

to choose how you want to think, going forward. This is where you can decide to let go of the thoughts that you have been having until now and choose thoughts that are more supportive of your well-being and the experiences that you desire to have. For example, if you have been thinking, "I am not good enough," now is the time to start deciding that you want to think something like, "I am good enough" or "I am capable."

Choosing your new thought patterns is the first step to finding a harmonious way of thinking. This way, you know what thoughts you want to have more, which becomes the thoughts that automatically comes to your head instead of the unhelpful or negative thoughts that you have been having so far. Once you identify a thought pattern that you want to dominate your mind at any situation, you need to start putting effort into actually transitioning your thought process. This part is easy; all you need to do is constantly catch yourself with your old thought pattern and push the positive thoughts in its place. Do this each time you notice yourself thinking about this particular topic. As you continue to swap your thoughts, you will find that the more desirable thought process begins to feel easier for you to agree with and believe in. It also begins to happen more naturally and automatically, replacing the old, negative thoughts that you were used to having. As this automatic transformation begins to happen, you will begin to see the positive effects of transforming your thoughts to the ones that are more mindful and positive.

Chapter 3

Creating a Strong Foundation

for Self-Esteem

Low self-esteem is an experience that many people in our modern society deal with. An estimated 80% of Americans deals with certain symptoms that relate to having low self-esteem. This means that only 20% of the population appears to have a strong sense of self-esteem. With more than two-thirds of the population suffering from low self-esteem, it makes sense that this is something that we need to address and find a solution for.

When it comes to addressing self-esteem, mindfulness is a powerful tool to aid the process. As you learned in Chapter 2, mindfulness can be a major contributing factor in helping people identify what their thought processes are and what mental patterns they tend to experience. It can also help you develop a deeper awareness around how you feel about yourself and the things that you experience in your life. This heightened awareness and understanding can be used to your advantage when it comes to cultivating a strong foundation for you to increase your sense of self-esteem and experience higher levels of self-confidence in your life.

In this chapter, we are going to discuss how you can use your transformed thought processes as a foundation to begin building your higher levels of self-esteem. With this, you will find the opportunity to use your thoughts directly as a way to improve how you feel about yourself and how you see yourself participating in the world around you. Although this does not necessarily mean that you are going to like every single aspect of who you are, it does mean that you are going to have a deeper sense of acceptance and compassion toward what makes you who you are, which makes cultivating higher self-esteem easier.

Become More Realistic

A major flaw in our modern society is the pressure we place on ourselves to becomea perfect, superhuman individual. Although social media and the internet has certainly made the experience more challenging, the truth is that we have been "keeping up with the Joneses" for generations. Humans are naturally competitive, and for many generations, we have learned to use that competitiveness to attempt to force ourselves in becoming better than everyone around us. Unfortunately, all that ends up happening is we find ourselves feeling worse every time we realize that we have a flaw or a weakness that we believe we shouldn't have. In the end, we find ourselves striving to reach unreasonable standards that we are never going to achieve because they are completely unrealistic.

Even those people who come across as uncaring toward what others think are known for struggling with these types of thoughts. These thoughts of trying to keep up with other people lead individuals to feel as if they are not good enough in many ways. Ultimately, they become hard on themselves in trying to force themselves to keep up with others. In the end, all we do is stigmatize what it means to be human while alienating ourselves and putting unreasonable pressure on ourselves, leading us to feel bad constantly.

When you allow yourself to become more realistic, you take a large amount of pressure off yourself and give yourself the opportunity to breathe and be human who is imperfect. You allow yourself more room to make mistakes, to accept yourself for your flaws, and to be understanding of your own weaknesses. As a result, you find yourself feeling more at peace just by lowering your expectations for who you are and who you should become. Believe it or not; lowering your expectations and your standards actually make it easier for you to grow, too, meaning, you are doing yourself a favor in many different ways by becoming more realistic.

An easy way to improve your ability to be more realistic

with yourself is to ask yourself, "if my loved one did this, would I think less of them?" In most cases, you will find that you are actually not nearly as bothered by lower standards as you think you are. In fact, many people find that they believe people who have lower standards and expectations are happier because they are not working so hard to assume an image or appearance that is unattainable. As a result, they live in freedom, and they feel more comfortable about their life overall.

Stay Present

While you improve your ability to be realistic with yourself about your expectations and experiences, you also need to focus on learning how you can stay present at the moment. Being present is one of the cornerstones of mindfulness, and it lends a great hand to help you improve your self-esteem and experience a more positive, confident, and enjoyable existence.

Being more present at the moment is going to help you in many ways. Primarily, it is going to support you in seeing each experience as an independent experience, rather than lumping them all together in your mind. Remember that your brain loves efficiency, and it will create a habitual way of thinking so that you have an easier time formulating thoughts and opinions about each new situation that you encounter. Although this impulse supports you in being more efficient, it can also lead you to have a more challenging time engaging in mindful thoughts in your everyday experiences. Many find themselves having thoughts where they link a current situation to a situation they experienced in the past, even though the two are not related in any way.

For example, if your friend in high school stole from you, and you find yourself struggling to trust friends going forward, there is a good chance that you are choosing thoughts based on memory rather than present experience. If you were to continue behaving in this way, then you would not be engaging in your relationships in a mindful manner. If, however, you were to identify that this thought came from past experience, you would have an easier time understanding that you were responding to memory rather than the present experience. This way, you could begin to make a thought transformation that would help you accept what happened in the past, and stay engaged at the present moment with more trust, effectively overcoming that negative thinking.

The more that you can stay at the present moment, the more you are going to be able to overcome all thoughts that link you back to your negative memories. This way, rather than remembering every time that someone did something wrong by you or said something mean to you, causing you to feel self-conscious and unworthy in new situations, you can engage in the new situation with more confidence and positivity. This means that rather than believing that every new person in your life is going to steal from you, think of you as unworthy, or believe that you are in any way "less" than who you should be, you can think that each new experience is just new. As a result, you will leave room for positive experiences, allowing you to enjoy your new encounters more thoroughly and without all of the stress and discomfort that comes from constantly worrying that something bad is going to happen.

Refrain From Judgment or Comparison

Judgment and comparison are two valuable tools that, when used properly, can help you in many different ways. For example, if you want to improve on a skill, you can look at someone who has more experience than you and compare your skills to theirs. This way, you can see exactly where you can improve and what needs to be done in order for you to improve and move toward a higher level of experience and skill. In this case, you are not comparing or judging with the intention to bully yourself into thinking that you are bad or that you have done something wrong. Instead, you are searching for opportunities for you to improve your skills so that you can become even better at what you are doing.

Unfortunately, many people do not use judgment and comparison exclusively for the opportunity to encourage themselves to improve. Instead, many use judgment and comparison as a way to prove that they are not good, worthy, or capable enough of doing something good in their lives. As a result, they find themselves feeling worse every single time they engage in judgment or comparison.

As you begin to move forward with the intention of mindfully improving your self-esteem, it is important that you learn to do so in a way that is free of toxic judgment and comparison. You need to learn how to look at other people or other people's actions without feeling like you are less than anyone else. Even if your skillset is lower or you have a weakness where other people have strength, this does not mean that you are not good enough or capable of the same activities. This does not mean that you are not worthy enough to be as loved or respected as they are. This is where realistic thinking can come in handy, too. The more that you think realistically, the more you are going to realize that you have plenty of qualities to be proud. You have more room to grow but not in a bad or negative way. Instead, you can grow as humans do, which is the realistic way.

When you do find yourself judging or comparing yourself against others according to your unrealistic standards, stop and engage in thought transformation techniques. Ask yourself if you ultimately believe that they are worthy of being judged or seen as less in any way, and follow that critical thought all the way to the end. In virtually every scenario, I guarantee that you will come to believe that the person you were initially judging does not deserve that judgment and, instead, deserves the benefit of the doubt and acceptance of who they are.

Be Mindful of Your Presentation

If you will recall, I mentioned previously that our emotions are the product of the thoughts that we have based on our environments. So, the way that we perceive our environment shapes the way that we think, thus shaping the emotions that we feel when we are in any given situation, such as entering a messy house that makes you feel stressed out as opposed to entering a cozy house that makes you feel comfortable. This experience can actually be used to help stimulate higher feelings of self-confidence and self-esteem by creating an environment or an experience where you are able to create thoughts that produce these positive feelings. Constantly practicing this fosters a higher self-confidence and self-esteem. The process of doing so is called "biofeedback."

Biofeedback essentially means that you create a physical experience that stimulates a specific thought, thus triggering a specific emotion. For example, when you are stressed out, and you go home and apply a face mask or drink a cup of hot tea, you are engaging in biofeedback by letting your body know that everything is okay. As a result, your perception of the present experience is that everything is okay, so emotionally, you are able to relax. This exact process can be used to encourage virtually anything, including heightened self-esteem and self-confidence.

When you are using biofeedback to improve your self-esteem and self-confidence, the best way to do so is to be mindful of your presentation. Psychologically speaking, we are largely impacted on a mental and emotional level by the posture we hold, the way that we dress, the way our faces look, and the way that we command the space that we are in. People who lack self-esteem and self-confidence often try to minimize their presentation in every way possible by displaying shrunken postures, wearing clothes that are ill-fitting to hide parts of them, keeping their faces neutral or as happy as possible, and taking up as little space as possible. Even just engaging in one or two of these behaviors can be indicative of low self-esteem, which can create negative feelings at certain times.

Instead, you want to improve your self-esteem by changing the way that you present yourself. You can do so by carrying a strong, tall, and confident posture where you keep your back straight, your shoulders down, and your head held high. At the same time, keep a facial expression that makes you feel most confident, and do not be afraid to use your facial expressions while communicating, as this helps improve your self-esteem and self-confidence about how you carry yourself when engaging with others. You also want to make sure that you are commanding your space, rather than trying to take up as little space as possible. Do not be afraid to let your elbows take up room when you are eating, to sit in a way that feels comfortable, and to keep your feet shoulder-width apart. The more that you command your space, the more confidence you are going to feel in the situation that you are partaking in. Finally, make sure that you dress in a way that makes you feel confident, too. This does not mean that you have to dress according to someone else's standards or in a way that makes someone else see you better than the way you are. Instead, you want to dress in a way that makes you feel confident because this is the approach that will help you be your best self.

The more that you learn to command your space, hold your body in a strong and confident manner, use your facial expressions, and dress in a way that makes you feel confident, the more you are telling yourself that you deserve to be confident and happy with yourself. As a result, biofeedback goes to work, and you find yourself having improved levels of self-esteem and self-confidence. As you continue to present yourself mindfully in this more confident way, you will find that it becomes easier for you to feel a heightened level of self-confidence and self-esteem, even when you are having a particularly challenging day.

Learn to Relax More

When it comes to creating a higher sense of self-esteem,

a great tool that you can take advantage of is relaxation. Each day, we are exposed to a large amount of stress in, which means that many people are living in a chronic state of fight or flight mode. If you do not take the time to create relaxation in your life, intentionally and mindfully, you struggle to create a state of inner peace, which results to feeling as if you are always stressed out, even when there seems to be no reason to be stressed out. Existing in this state can lead you to feel on edge and overwhelmed all the time. It can make you feel as if you are excessively aware of what is going on around you. This means that you are more fixated on everything, making it easier for you to judge, complain, and generally feel negative about everything that is going on around you. It also leads you to become hyper-aware and conscious of what you are doing and how other people are looking at you. This means that you notice every "strange" look or glance you receive from other people. To make it short, this entails being stressed out on a regular basis, which can lead you to feel like the entire world thinks something is wrong with you. Sometimes, you feel as if, maybe, they are right.

Learning how to step out of this negativity in your head

is crucial if you want to help yourself improve your sense of self-esteem. You need to learn how to relax completely so that you can stop having these highly uncomfortable experiences that lead you to have even lower levels of self-confidence and self-esteem.

Relaxing completely is a behavior that is best done with the aid of mindfulness. Learning to relax completely means that you need to become mindful and aware of how you currently experience stress and what you can do to eliminate the thoughts that bring you stress. This is a great opportunity to use your mindful thinking skills to become aware of what your thoughts are and how they are affecting your mood and stress levels. Then, you can begin to become aware of how your body feels and what type of stressors you are carrying within your body, allowing you to identify the opportunity to release these stressors.

Begin to Act "As If"

Another thing that you can do to begin improving your self-esteem and self-confidence mindfully is to act "as if." This behavior works for the same reason that biofeedback works, and that is by allowing to carry yourself as if you do feel confident. This sends a message to your brain that you are feeling confident and that you have improved self-esteem, and as a result, you start feeling that way. In addition to paying attention to how you are presenting yourself, you can also choose to pay attention to how you are behaving and acting when you are in new situations. Acting as though you already have a heightened sense of confidence and self-esteem, even if you do not, can help you begin to feel as if you do. Soon, you will begin to behave with that heightened level of self-confidence and self-esteem automatically, and you will not have to put in so much effort to feel this increased sense of confidence.

One good way to act in a more confident manner is to use visualization as a tool to support you. You can spend a few minutes a day visualizing what you want to look like, feel like, and behave if you had increased confidence and increased self-esteem. This would help you get a strong understanding of projecting an image of confidence. Studies have shown that spending just 10 minutes a day invested in active visualization meditation can help you completely change the way that you live your life and the way that you approach the world around you. This happens because you are tricking your brain into believing that you already have acted this way in a real-life scenario since your brain does not actually know the difference between a memory, a visualization, and a real-life experience.

Chapter 4

Meditation and Mindfulness

Oftentimes, meditation and mindfulness are discussed hand-in-hand, leading to many people not realizing that there is actually a difference between the two. This connection might arise due to the fact that there is a form of meditation known as "mindful meditation," and it is intended to bridge the two so that you can use meditation as a tool to cultivate a deeper sense of mindfulness in your life.

When it comes to awakening through mindfulness and improving your personal growth and self-esteem, understanding how each of these two tools serves you and how they can fit together to serve each other is important. Recognizing when, where, and how each one can be used is going to help you learn which tool is necessary for the job at hand, allowing you to create change effectively in your life in many different ways. Throughout this chapter, we are going to cover what each tool is, when you should use that tool, and how you can use it in such a way that it is going to give you the best results.

The Differences between
Meditation and Mindfulness

The biggest difference between meditation and mindfulness is where your awareness resides when you are using mindfulness or meditation as a tool and how you can use that awareness to achieve a specific result. In meditation, while you use mindfulness to help improve your practice, your primary focus is within yourself. You are focused largely on how you are feeling, what is going on inside of your body, and what thoughts you are having in your mind. Meditation is entirely focused on your experience with the world around you and how that is affecting you. Mindfulness, on the other hand, is external. With mindfulness, you are focusing on how you are experiencing the world as you perceive it, what is going on around you, and how you are being impacted by events or circumstances that are beyond your physical self.

In many cases, these two tools are interchangeable, and you can use both at the same time. In doing so, you allow yourself to turn your awareness both inward and outward, achieving a greater state of understanding of what is going on inside your head and what is going on around you and elsewhere in the world. Having both of these elements in your consciousness helps create a fuller sense of understanding of every area of your life. This way, you can create more mindful and intentional approaches to the world around you.

Everything You Need to Know
About Using Meditation

Meditation itself is generally done in a seated or lying

down position so that the individual can remain still and focused on their inner world. Virtually every time you engage in meditation, you are also engaging in some degree of inward mindfulness, allowing you to increase your focus on what is going on inside your head. In common meditation practices, your focus is largely on expanding your awareness, creating a state of calmness within yourself, and finding inner peace. You spend your time relaxing, breathing, and being one with yourself so that you can begin to have more integrated and peaceful experience with life itself.

There are countless types of meditation that you can engage in, each with its own set of benefits that can help you in one way or another. If you want to live a more mindful and awakened life, understanding each of these types of meditation and how they work is important. Each meditation type is going to be a tool that you can use at one point or another in your life, so it is worthwhile to understand what they are and when you can use them.

The first type of meditation that you may want to use is

known as "breath-awareness meditation," and it also happens to be the most basic and common form of meditation that you can perform. Breath-awareness meditation helps you relax by allowing you to focus solely on your breath and the way your body feels each time you inhale or exhale. Many people use breath-awareness meditation on a day to day basis as a way to keep themselves relaxed and more resilient toward stressors and discomforts that life brings.

"Loving-kindness meditation" is another form of meditation that you can practice. This type of meditation allows its practitioners to send love and kindness to themselves, other people in their lives, and the world at large. It also allows you to internalize anything that you currently experience. The purpose of loving-kindness meditation is to teach yourself to have a more loving, kind, compassionate, and understanding approach to the world around you. This is a powerful form of meditation for people who find themselves frequently feeling frustrated, upset, or angry because of the different stressors that they may be experiencing in their everyday lives.

"Mantra-based meditation" is a meditation style that can help you create certain feelings within yourself and your body. Mantras are often chosen by the meditating individual based on their goal of helping themselves create a certain focus or state of awareness within. Some mantras are simple, humming sounds that have been used traditionally for generations as a way to create stillness and calmness within the body. Other mantras are affirmations that the individual chooses to repeat to themselves as a way to help them stimulate more feelings of empowerment, compassion, love, peace, calmness, affection, confidence, beauty, acceptance, or anything positivity that they desire more in their lives.

"Visualization meditations" are used for many reasons, although they are typically used to help people prepare themselves for new or significant life experiences. For example, if you are preparing for an important career meeting that you have been waiting for, visualization can help you prepare yourself for the meeting by giving yourself a clear focus of what you want to accomplish and how you are going to accomplish it. You can also use visualization to improve your skills, socialization abilities, confidence or self-esteem, your happiness, and many other things. You can also use it to attain and maintain overall peace in your life.

"Guided meditations" are used for many different experiences. Its benefits overlap with that of visualization meditations. You can use guided meditation to improve your inner peace, help you sleep, prepare you for something important, or even to visualize what you want more in your life using a tool called "manifesting." Guided meditations can be used by following a guided YouTube meditation or audio meditation or by visiting a meditation specialist who can guide you through a live in-person session as you meditate.

When it comes to meditation, you need to be prepared to set aside some time for your meditative experience. This way, you have enough time, energy, and attention to engage in your meditation and gain your desired benefits from it. You should always have an intention or goal when going through your meditation experience, as this will help keep you focused and give you a reason for showing up in your meditation sessions. The reason for meditating for many is as simple as "I want to feel more relaxed right now." Having a reason for engaging in your meditation helps you create a purpose that you can be mindful of, allowing you to integrate mindfulness into your meditation experience. As a result, no matter what form of meditation you engage in, you will also be actively exercising and strengthening your mindfulness abilities.

Everything You Need to Know
About Using Mindfulness

Mindfulness is entirely focused on your state of awareness and where you place your focus. This includes the practice of meditation itself, but it also includes your everyday life and the experiences that you have about the world. Being in an active state of mindfulness ultimately means that you are focusing on your thoughts, feelings, behaviors, and movements. You are also focusing on how you are affecting the world around you and how the world around you is affecting you.

You can engage in a mindfulness practice anytime, regardless of where you are, who you are surrounded by, and what is going on around you. When you are being mindful, you are paying attention and noticing everything about the present moment, regardless of whether or not you perceive it to be good or bad. This is a powerful state to be in, as it differs from how the average person lives their day to day lives. Most people go through their lives mechanically and doing

71

everything because they have to and because it is what they have always done. They succumb to their efficient brains and habits, and then they simply engage in these habits over and over again. This way, rather than having to put the energy and effort into actively thinking about what they are doing, they can just do it on autopilot and let their minds be at rest as they go about their day. For a person who is being mindful, this looks entirely different.

When you choose to be mindful, you choose to engage in all of your daily experiences even if you have been doing them for years. This means that you become aware of what you are experiencing, what is going on around you, how you are affecting the situation, and how the situation is affecting you. Creating this active engagement in your present experience means that your mind has the capacity to stay clearly focused on what you are doing, rather than wandering as you engage in life on autopilot. As a result, you live a much more integrated, enjoyable, and present life. You also experience a greater sense of security, comfort, and peace because you can feel confident about every move and decision that you make, rather than doing it all from memory.

It can be challenging for the human mind to find time to engage in mindfulness.According to a study, humans spend roughly 46.9% of their waking hours thinking about things beyond what they are actively doing. This means that you really have to work toward engaging your mind and bringing it back to the present moment so that you can have a more positive, present, and integrated experience in your life. Using mindfulness during your everyday life helps you combat this activity so that you can begin to stay more actively engaged in what you are doing each day.

Just as I have mentioned previously, you want to be using mindfulness as often as you can. The best way to determine whether or not you need to employ mindfulness as a tool actively is to gauge how integrated you are in your day-to-day activities. If you find that you are not overly focused or aware of what you are doing and how you are doing it, then you need to begin practicing mindfulness. This way, you can integrate yourself more deeply, and you can get the most out of the experience. This also reduces the amount of stress that you are feeling mentally and physically.

Bridging the Gap with Mindfulness Meditation

Bridging the gap between mindfulness and meditation can be done by engaging in a type of meditation known as mindfulness meditation. Mindfulness meditation is a meditation style where the individual focuses their entire session solely on becoming as mindful in the experience as they possibly can. A popular mindfulness meditation style that has been used in many therapies and treatments is known as the raisin meditation, as we have mentioned earlier. This involves eating a raisin with mindfulness. You could do this meditation with any small snack item, ranging from a chip to a chocolate bar, and you can even switch it up between what you are using from time to time if you really want to engage in mindfulness each time. Regardless of what you are going to be eating, however, the meditation remains the same. The goal of mindfulness eating meditations is always eating in the most engaging and active way that is possible. You want to focus on what the food looks like, what it feels like in your hands, and what it smells like. Then, you want to take time to focus on how it feels in your mouth, what it tastes like, and how the texture or taste changes as you begin to chew on that food item. When you swallow, pause to think about how that felt and the lingering taste in your mouth. This eating style engages your mindfulness in every way possible, making it a highly enjoyable, engaged, and integrated experience. The benefit of engaging in mindful eating meditations is that it helps you learn about how you can mindfully become aware of your body and the way that your senses interact with the outer world. This way, you have a clearer understanding of how you experience the world around you and what those experiences tend to feel like for you.

You can also engage in mindfulness meditation using what is known as a body scan or progressive muscle relaxation. In this particular meditation style, your goal is to identify each part of your body and mindfully relax it so that you feel your body more at peace. Typically, with body scan meditations, you will start at your feet and work your way up and then continue until you reach your head. As you do this exercise, you mindfully become aware of each body part along the way, including how it feels and how you can help it relax more deeply. Engaging in this experience helps you become more mindfully aware of your own body and how your own body feels, allowing you to have a deeper understanding of it. It also allows you to connect with your physical body. When it comes to creating a strong relationship with your body and a deeper awareness of how your body feels and works, this is a powerful practice to use. Having a strong awareness can help you in many ways, including having a deeper understanding of what your body needs in order to feel healthy and comfortable.

Mindfulness meditation is a powerful tool that bridges the benefits of both of these tools, giving you the opportunity to both relax and find peace while also increasing your mindful experiences in life. Ideally, you should incorporate mindfulness meditation into your life by practicing it at least two or three times a week. In doing so, you are going to help yourself mindfully awaken and enjoy life in a more peaceful and confident manner. This will not only help you feel better at the moment, but it will also improve your ability to be mindful in other more practical areas of your life.

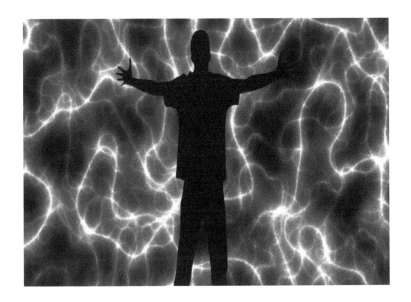

Chapter 5

Developing a Meditation Routine

Although meditation and mindfulness have notable differences, using meditation as a part of your mindfulness development is ideal. Meditation is a tool that directly improves your ability to be mindful, so using it on a daily basis or at least multiple times per week can help you have an easier time living a mindful life overall.

Exploring how you can work a meditation routine into your life and what you need to do in order to create a meditation routine that serves your mindfulness is crucial. This way, you can create a meditation routine that is going to improve your awakening further, increase your confidence and self-esteem, empower you, improve your personal growth, and help you feel happier and lighter in general. There are many ways where you can incorporate a meditation routine into your life, so in this chapter, we are going to explore several factors that you can consider when creating your personalized routine. This way, you can design a meditation routine that is going to suit your needs perfectly, allowing you to design one that is really going to help you improve your mindfulness and the quality of your life.

Creating a meditation routine according to your unique needs is not only a great way to create a tool that you can use to create more mindfulness and peace in your life, but it is also a great way to actively use your mindfulness tools to create an experience that is ideal for you. As you create your own routine, you are going to tap into your current mindfulness skills so that you can identify what your needs are, how your meditation routine can best serve you, and what you can do to make it even more powerful and enjoyable. Below, I will walk you through the steps of understanding your own needs and desires so that you can customize a meditation routine that will change your entire approach to life.

Create Your Meditation Goal

The first thing you want to do when it comes to creating your own meditation routine is to create a goal for yourself. In this case, your goal may be that you want to become more mindful and that you want to create a deeper awareness of the life that you are living. You may make any number of goals, however. You can include goals such as the need to relax more, the ease of navigating daily stress, andbetter emotional management. Your goal is personal to you, so make sure that you pick something that is truly meaningful to you. This way, you can feel confident that you are creating a goal that is going to help keep your motivation to meditate constantly and improve your mindfulness abilities as you go along your routine.

Choose the Meditation Style That Suits Your Needs

After you have chosen your meditation goal, you need to choose a meditation style that is going to help you reach your goal and meet your needs. Each of the meditation styles that were described earlier is capable of helping you achieve different needs, so it would be a great idea to choose one that is going to help you with a specific goal that you have set for yourself. If you have a goal other than mindfulness, you should also choose to use a form of mindfulness meditation so that you are able to improve your mindfulness in your day to day life. It is important to understand that you can certainly alternate between meditation styles when you are developing a routine for yourself. In fact, for many people, alternating between meditation styles improves their ability to stay mindful of their meditation experience because they are consistently focusing on something slightly different.

Mindfully Work it Into Your Schedule

Once you have identified what meditation style is going to suit your needs, you need to determine how you are going to work your meditation routine into your schedule so that you can engage with it on a regular basis. This is a wonderful opportunity for you to practice mindfulness, as this is a chance for you to determine when you have enough time, energy, and desire to engage in a consistent meditation routine. To do this, sit and consider what part of the day you have the easiest time sitting down to relax and engage in meditation, as this is going to be the time that you want to use for your meditation practice. You also want to consider what part of the day you are uninterrupted by tasks and people around you. You do not want to set aside time to meditate only to be interrupted, especially when you are already deep into the practice. Once you have set the time of day that you think is going to work for you, you want to begin meditating on that schedule every day. If you find that you are not meditating well because of your schedule, like not having enough time as you initially thought or having tasks that chase you despite the time you set aside for yourself, then you can

85

always adapt your schedule to adjust to your needs. Having to do so will only give you the opportunity to know yourself and your needs even better while also having the opportunity to adapt your approach so that you can continue to meditate on a regular basis.

Discover a Way to Make it Better

When you are ready to engage in meditation actively, you need to find ways where you can make it better for yourself. One of the best parts of meditation is that it is largely about you and your desire to feel more relaxed and engaged at the present moment with yourself. This means that you can make it all about you. Before you actually begin to meditate, take the time to understand what you can do to make your meditation even more peaceful. Because you want to improve your mindfulness, a great way to decide how you can make your meditation even better is to consider each of your senses as they are a part of your meditation experience. You want to choose a meditation space where you will feel most comfortable and engaged in your meditation. This could mean sitting at a park and enjoying the cool breeze against your skin while also having a beautiful

86

view and the sounds of the park, or it could mean sitting in a comfortable room in your home with a soft blanket, burning candles, and gentle music in the background. Use this as an opportunity to get to know yourself better so that you can identify what helps you feel most relaxed and then use those things to improve your meditation experience. This will not only help you meditate better, but it will also help you enjoy the experience even more, which means that you will be likely to continue engaging in the experience.

Engagein Your New Routine

With everything in place, all you need to do is start engaging in your new routine. Early on, many people start with great intentions but then quickly find themselves failing to continue their practice for a number of reasons. It is not uncommon to decide that you are too busy or uninterested in it or that the benefits that you stand to gain are not actually that important to you and what you desire. The more that you engage in your meditation practice, the more that it becomes a habit and therefore, the easier it will be for you to continue your practice. This way, you can stop making up excuses and reasons for not meditating, and you can continue with your practice.

Mindfully Improve it Over Time

When it comes to creating new practices in our lives, it is important to understand that what we think will work for us and what actually works for us are often two different things. As you begin to engage in your meditation practice, you will likely find that certain things need to be altered or adjusted in order for you to have your best possible experience. You might also find that your goal or the reasoning behind your goal can shift over time, as you begin to understand yourself on a deeper level. It is important that you allow yourself to adapt your practice as needed so that you are always engaging in a practice that serves your true needs. Although it is ideal to be disciplined and engaged in the same practice every day, this does not mean that you cannot change the details of the practice to help it better suit your needs.

Chapter 6

Becoming More Mindful in Your Life

Until now, we have placed a large focus on creating an experience of mindfulness from within. Many of the tools that we have covered are focused on creating a deeper sense of self-awareness and self-acceptance so that you can feel more confident in yourself as you go through life. This is important, as the way that you feel about yourself and how you perceive yourself in life largely contributes to how you carry yourself in life, and what you do with your life.

As you improve your self-esteem and increase your self-confidence, you also want to make sure that you are using mindfulness to change the way that you live and experience your life. By incorporating mindfulness into your everyday activities, you give yourself the opportunity to improve your self-esteem further while also giving yourself a wonderful opportunity to enjoy life at an even deeper level. Through this, you will find that you feel better with yourself as a person and in the life that you choose to live. Many find that this is the point where they begin to feel liberated from the stressors of day to day life in modern society because they give themselves the opportunity to enjoy more mental and emotional peace even when surrounded by things that previously created stress.

There are many opportunities where you have to incorporate more mindfulness into your daily life, but we are going to discuss six of them here. These six strategies can be incorporated into every single day of your life so that you have the capacity to live your best life while also making mindfulness part of your "default setting." In other words, the more you can incorporate it into your everyday activities, the easier it will be for you to remember to engage in mindfulness because it becomes a part of everything that you do.

Wake Up and Be Mindful

A great time of day for you to practice mindfulness is upon waking up. When we were children, many of us heard the expression, "did you wake up on the wrong side of the bed?" This ultimately means, "did you wake up with a bad mood?" And believe it or not, this expression has more weight to it than many of us originally believed it did. When we wake up, our first thoughts can have a huge impact on the way that the rest of our days go. If we wake up dreading the day ahead or feeling upset in any way about our tasks, it can make us feel stressed out and frustrated for the rest of the day. Alternatively, if we wake up feeling refreshed, peaceful, and excited for what lies ahead, we can feel confident that our underlying attitude toward the day will be peaceful, exciting, and with room for curiosity.

You can actually shape your first thoughts of the day by making it a habit to wake up and be mindful right from the moment you open your eyes. You can do so by creating a mindful routine that you engage in as soon as you wake up so that these thoughts are habitual, which means that you habitually wake up in a great mood. An excellent routine that you can mindfully engage in immediately upon awakening includes waking up and expressing gratitude for the thighs you may feel grateful for. You might feel gratitude toward your life, the lives of the people you love, and the activities that you will partake in that day or anything else that helps you genuinely feel grateful. In doing so, you wake up with an attitude of feeling grateful, which means that you are far more likely to feel optimistic, kind, and joyful throughout the rest of the day, all because of one simple mindfulness exercise that you practiced as soon as you woke up.

Be Mindful About Your Routines

Earlier, I mentioned how many people go through their day to day lives on autopilot, shifting from one activity to the next, without much thought, and never fully engaging in what they do. Much of their activities are encoded in muscle memory and habit and do not seem to require them to pay attention or be present in the activity itself. This, obviously, is not a sign of mindfulness and can drastically reduce your ability to partake in mindfulness throughout your everyday activities. Instead, you want to engage in mindfulness by being more actively aware of the activities that you perform, even if such activities have been part of your routine for a long period of time.

Focus on mindfully bringing your awareness back to everything from how you brush your teeth in the morning to your daily commute and even the way that you eat your lunch at break time. Take mundane, everyday tasks and turn them into mindfulness rituals that you engage in while you go through your daily life, and see just how mindful you can truly become. As you do this, you can also find out if there are new strategies

95

that you can use to make your routines more purposeful, effective, or enjoyable for you each day. This way, you know that everything you are doing is mindful, intentional, and supportive in helping you live your best life possible.

Set Time for a Wandering Mind

As humans, our minds love to wander. We have been daydreaming since the day we were born; we stare into space and allow our minds to be filled with wonderful thoughts, opinions, feelings, and experiences that each of us constantly has. Letting your mind wander is not a bad thing. In fact, daydreaming is healthy and can even improve your overall sense of well-being by minimizing the level of stress that you carry with you on a daily basis. That being said, it is important that you are more mindful and intentional when you let your mind wander so that you do not interrupt important activities with a wandering mind.

A great way to nurture your mind's desire to wander while also keeping it focused when needed is by setting

96

time for a wandering mind. Each day, set time aside for you to sit back and just let your mind roam freely, thinking about whatever you want. Put your phone down, turn off the TV, set down your book, and do nothing but stare at the wall and enjoy a few minutes of silence. As you do, let your mind wander anywhere without trying to influence, manipulate, or judge any of the thoughts that enter your mind as it wanders. If you need to, you can do this every hour or two as a way to give yourself a "brain break," as this may help you be more engaged and focused during your everyday experiences afterward.

Keep Your Activities Short

Our minds are not known for being focused for long periods of time. In fact, studies have suggested that we have our best focus for about 20 minutes, and then after that, we find ourselves losing focus on what we are doing. If you want to improve your mindfulness and allow yourself to be as engaged as possible in everything that you are doing, seek to set the intention of focusing for 20 minutes at a time before giving yourself a brain break by going to the bathroom, letting your mind wander, or drinking a glass of water. Chunking your activities down into shorter bursts and respecting your brain's natural tendency to lose focus after 20 minutes actually improves your ability to stay mindful and focused throughout the day. This way, rather than attempting to force your brain to keep going, you are working with its natural behavior. As a result, your brain understands what you want from it and has an easier time helping you stay mindfully engaged for each of the 20-minute bursts.

Be Mindful While You Are Waiting

Our society seems to wait a lot. We wait in line, we wait at red lights, we wait for our lunch break, we wait for the workday to be over, and we wait for a lot of things. Waiting is a natural part of life, and even if our society was structured in any other way, we would still find ourselves waiting consistently. That being said, waiting is a great time for you to begin practicing mindfulness and engaging more deeply into the present moment. As you wait for things in life, give yourself time to do a mindfulness check.

A great strategy to use during this time is the 5-4-3-2-1 mindfulness strategy, which helps you become mindful and present in your environment in a fairly short period. You can do this by simply finding 5 things to observe visually, 4 things to touch, 3 things to hear, 2 things to smell, and 1 thing to taste. This way, you engage your entire sensory body into the mindfulness experience as you are waiting. If you want to set yourself up for success with this practice, you can keep a pack of gum or a bottled drink with you whenever you expect that you will be waiting, as this will give you something to engage your sense of taste with.

Choose a Mindfulness Trigger

One great way to improve your mindfulness is by creating a mindfulness trigger. A mindfulness trigger is ultimately a prompt that is going to remind you that you need to engage in mindfulness practice. This way, anytime you see or interact with this prompt, your mind immediately begins to look for opportunities to engage in mindfulness and tune in with the present moment.

Your mindfulness trigger can be anything from a specific color to a specific object, or even a specific time of day. When that trigger is set off, all you need to do is intentionally engage in your mindfulness check-in for a few moments so that you can train your brain that this is what the trigger is prompting you to do. At first, it will take some effort on your part to remember that this is what the prompt is for and to respond to the trigger properly. However, as you continue to use your trigger to remind you to engage in mindfulness, you will find yourself having a more effective mindfulness practice revolving around your new trigger.

Chapter 7

Powerful Habit Changes

for a Better Life

You are now fully aware of just how much our brains rely on habits to get us through our daily lives. You have also come to understand how you can use such habits to help you have a better quality of life by creating habits that are going to help you become more mindful in your everyday existence. Now, it is time for you to understand how you can create, shift, and adapt your existing habits to become even more mindful.

Leveraging your habits as a way to improve mindfulness

is a powerful opportunity for you to work closely with your brain's natural tendencies so that you can experience even more mindfulness in your everyday life. When it comes to making changes in your life, especially when it comes to the way that you live your life or the lifestyle that you lead, it is important to know how you can work together with your natural behavior to make those changes last longer. A big mistake that many people make when they are trying to make a huge lifestyle change is that they try to change the very fibers of who they are. In many cases, they even try to change the way their mind and body naturally works, which ultimately fails in the end because it is extremely difficult to go against your natural tendencies. Rather than putting so much effort in changing the way that you are, you can work together with your natural tendencies to create systems within yourself that work more effectively to help you live the life that you desire. These types of changes are easier to make, and they end up being more sustainable and longer-lasting in the long run because they are simple adaptations ofthe things that you have already been doing all along.

The chances are, you have many habits that influence the way that you live your life and the experiences that you have. We all tend to have habits around the same things in our lives, though what those habits are and how we engage with them vary from person to person. For example, we all have a habit on how we start our day, but the actual details of that habit are different, depending on who you are and the habits that you developed throughout your life. In this chapter, we are going to explore some of these common habits that we all have and how you can create habits and rituals that are going to suit your needs. As we delve into these things, I want you to remember that the emphasis will always be on adjusting *your* personal habits to suit what you are trying to achieve, rather than attempting to discard your habits entirely and start fresh. Again, adapting what you are already doing will always be more efficient than trying to create entirely new habits from scratch, so do not be afraid to make changes. You might need to adopt a small number of your habits at a time and gradually shift them to become desirable habits in a way that they last long. No matter what you have to do to make these changes work, trust that you are doing it in the right way for yourself. You just have to listen to your body and your personal needs as you go.

Your Morning Habits

All of us have habits that we engage in each morning, right from the minute we wake up and until we officially start our first task of the day, such as leaving for work or class. Your morning habits can have a huge impact on your everyday life, as you already know, so having a strong set of habits that you engage in each morning can help you have a better day by improving your mood and helping you achieve more throughout the day.

Your morning routine is a great opportunity for you to create mindful habits that are going to help you set the rest of your day in positivity. When it comes to creating a mindful morning routine for yourself, it is helpful to consider what needs to be accomplished in order for you to get the most out of your routine. Each person is going to need something different based on what they do every day. For example, if you have a career that starts early in the day and requires high physical exertion, you are going to need to wake up early and have a nourishing routine that helps prepare you for a day of physical work. Alternatively, if you have a career that requires you to work from home, you are going to need to have a morning routine that motivates you to get started so that you can get the job done. Knowing what you need from your morning routine is going to help you ensure that all the elements of your routine are geared toward helping you get started with your day in the best way possible.

Once you know what you need from your morning routine, it is ideal to create an outline of what you would like to accomplish. Be mindful of what you need, the things that you enjoy in your morning routine, as well as the details of your current routine. All these pieces of information will contribute to making good choices when establishing a new routine. With this in mind, consider how your current routine could be adapted to suit your needs and set you up for success for the rest of your day. Then, begin engaging in this routine on a daily basis so that you can start gaining the benefits of this routine and further adapting it to suit your needs and preferences.

Your Cooking and Eating Habits

In our society, cooking and eating have become habits

that we do not really think about. In the past, it was customary for everyone to sit down to a home-cooked meal together with the family and enjoy a conversation about how each other's day went and how their day could have gone better. These days, meals are not really thought about in most households, and people do not sit down to enjoy them together like they once did. Furthermore, convenience has become customary in many homes, resulting in people eating low-quality fast foods and convenience-store foods rather than eating healthier home-cooked meals. As a result, eating has become more of a chore than a ritual that people engage in to nourish their bodies and take care of their well-being.

Transforming your own cooking and eating habits to become more mindful is a great opportunity for you to reclaim this part of your day and transform both cooking and eating into a more enjoyable activity. By addressing your cooking and eating habits properly, you can create a healthier lifestyle while also becoming more mindfully engaged in your cooking and eating routines. A great way to get started is to plan out each meal intentionally. As you cook, focus on being fully present in the experience of cooking so that you can truly engage with the activity and enjoy the peace and quiet of the experience.

When you are ready to eat, make sure that you eat mindfully. Consider the mindful meditation with the raisin, as we have discussed before, and do the same when you are eating the food that you have cooked for yourself. Eat slowly, and enjoy the appearance, smell, and texture of the food.Take your time enjoying every single bite. After you finish your meal, take some time to enjoy how it feels and the aftertaste of your meal. The more that you enjoy each part of the eating experience, the better you are going to enjoy each meal, and the more peaceful you are going to feel in your everyday life.

Your Hygienic Habits

Each of us has to maintain hygienic habits every single day in order to maintain our health. From brushing our teeth and combing our hair to showering and clipping our nails, there are many hygienic habits that we all engage in so that we can take care of our bodies and stay healthy. These habits cannot be drastically altered because they are basic habits, but they can certainly be made more enjoyable so that you have a positive time taking care of your body rather than feeling burdened to look after your well-being.

A great way to begin turning your hygienic habits into healthy, enjoyable habits is to see each experience as one that is devoted to taking care of yourself. People who genuinely enjoy in self-care enjoy activities centered around hygiene because it helps them truly dedicate some non-negotiable time to themselves and the way that they feel. During this time, they pamper their bodies and, as a result, their minds. By giving themselves a few minutes of und evoted attention for the sole purpose of taking care of themselves, one becomes mindful even when it's as simple as combing

110

the hair. For many people, this is a refreshing opportunity to take care of themselves.

You can make your hygiene habits more mindful by slowing down and enjoying them more thoroughly. Use this as an opportunity to get to know your body and spend more time properly looking after your body and appreciating it and yourself for all that you are. Rather than rushing through a habitual process that may or may not still fit your hygienic needs, slow down and make sure that each part of the process is being done properly and is thoroughly satisfying your body's needs. You will probably find that the deeper you can immerse yourself into this self-care practice, the more relaxed you are going to feel, in addition to feeling satisfied with your self-care activities. This stems from slowing down and listening to your body, which means that it has time to work out naturally and release any stress or anxiety. Furthermore, you can take advantage of biofeedback at this point and use relaxing self-care practices that teach your body that it is safe to feel comfortable and relaxed, which will naturally help ease up any stress or anxiety that you may be experiencing.

Your Work Habits

We all have habits revolving around our working experiences that contribute to how we show up to work, how we partake in our daily activities, and how we complete the stuff that we are expected to complete on a day-to-day basis. When it comes to your work habits, knowing what your habits are and how they are serving your success is important. For many people, unless their habits have been addressed and they choose to create healthier habits for their work-life mindfully, they find themselves actually creating and engaging in habits that are likely to hold them back from achieving any significant level of success in their career. This is because the mind craves efficiency and slacking certainly seems to be the most efficient way to make it through the day without exerting too much energy or expecting too much from ourselves.

When it comes to your own work habits, it can be hard to admit to yourself whether or not you are slacking at work, especially if you think that you should take pride in the work that you do. That being said, it is important that you are honest with yourself when your behavior is holding you back from achieving greater success in your career. This way, you can begin to create new habits that are going to help you excel and achieve your work goals while also feeling less stressed over your journey to success.

After you have honestly addressed what needs to be done for you to have greater success in your career, you need to begin identifying habits that are going to help you become more successful. These habits could be anything from showing up to work early to starting your daily tasks right away. Good habits can also include putting a greater effort into every report that you write, completing meticulously every project assigned to you, and submitting the highest quality of work to your superior. As you create these new habits, be mindful of how you are affected by the habits and how they benefit you. Having this mindfulness will help you create new habits that are going to serve you for years to come while also helping you remain engaged in the present moment as you carry out these mindful habits.

Your Hobby and Fun Habits

In our society, a common habit that people have developed is engaging in their hobbies as a way to bypass the stress that they experience in their lives. People binge-watch TV for hours on end, play video games for far too many hours, and obsess over their hobbies and certain forms of entertainment as an opportunity to cope with the stress that comes from work or elsewhere in their lives. While hobbies and fun activities can certainly help lower stress levels, they should not be used to avoid stress. At best, they should be used as a temporary distraction to help you relax before going back to doing the tasks that cause stress to identify a long-term solution and move forward in a more intentional manner.

When it comes to creating habits around your hobbies and the activities that you find to be fun, the first habit that you need to address is the reason for engaging in these hobbies. If you pursue these hobbies and activities to create genuine fun and maintain a healthier state of mind, then there is nothing that you truly need to address or change in your activities. If you are engaging in your hobbies and fun experiences because you are trying to avoid dealing with other more challenging parts of your life, however, you need to address the trigger that is causing you to engage in those hobbies. In this case, you need to create a new trigger that encourages you to engage in your hobbies, as well as a new habit that allows you to cope with stress elsewhere in your life. This way, when you pursue your hobbies and enjoy fun activities, you are doing so mindfully and in a way that allows you to immerse in the experience. This is in contrast to pursuing these activities because you are running away from something else.

Another way to improve your habits around your hobbies is to ensure that you are scheduling a time for these experiences on a regular basis. If you do not, you tend to find a way to squeeze them in your schedule, even if you do not actually have enough time for them. This results in feeling even more stressed out. Having adequate time to engage in your hobbies and to have fun means that you can fully become present at the moment and enjoy those fun experiences.

Allowing yourself to immerse into your hobbies fully means that you can truly let go of everything else going on in your life and fully engage in the process of fun without feeling like you are avoiding anything in your life. This way, you can be mindful of each step in the process and deeply enjoy the entire experience.

Your Alone Time Habits

The last habit that you really need to address when it comes to creating healthier habits that support your mindfulness would be your alone time habits. Alone time is a vital experience that we all need to have in our lives to give ourselves the opportunity to experience relief from the external world. This is our time to relax, step away from our environment, and simply enjoy spending time alone with ourselves. Although some people claim not to enjoy this, psychologists argue that alone time is crucial in helping us live our lives as fully independent and happy human beings. People who know how to be alone and enjoy that time tend to be happier because they do not rely on other people, things, or circumstances to feel happy.

Creating habits around spending more time alone, doing what you love, and genuinely relaxing away from the rest of the world are all important. Even if you are only spending an hour or two each week doing something that you love, you are nurturing this part of yourself that needs to experience this independence and space away from others. This way, you are able to recalibrate and feel more appreciative and thankful for the people around you. Furthermore, your body and brain have the opportunity to relax fully and release the feelings of overstimulation that can come from spending too much time around other people and stressful activities. As a result, you will feel a lot less edgy and stressed out around other people in your life when you get to recharge, and you will have an easier time mindfully enjoying the time that you spend with others, too.

When you do engage in this alone time, put effort into making the entire experience about enjoying a more mindful moment. Pay attention to how you feel, your needs, and the activities that you can pursue so that you can thoroughly fulfill your needs and feel a lot more satisfied and less stressed. You might find that, sometimes, your alone time is best spent laying on the couch relaxing, while other times, you might want to go for a walk or get a drink from your favorite café. Your time alone may also be spent reading, playing your favorite game, or just looking at the sky and enjoying a peaceful moment. Regardless of what you need, taking the time to listen to your body and fulfill your needs is going to help you make your alone time more enjoyable while also mindfully using it to destress and create a greater sense of well-being in your life.

Chapter 8

Learning to Declutter Your Life

Our lives are filled with more than we need, and this has only gotten worse as we have matured as a consumerist society. We are constantly bringing more into our lives than we need, which can create a massive amount of stress in our lives. If you have never taken the time to declutter every aspect of your life mindfully, the chances are, you are engaging in a life that has become overwhelmed by too many details.

Part of living a more mindful life is having a purpose or an intention behind everything that you do, everything that you have, and everything that you acquire. The meaning behind why you do something needs to be meaningful enough to validate why you are doing it. If it is not meaningful enough, there is a chance that it is not helping you live your best life, so it is ideal for you to let go of such things, allowing you to have more space in your life for the things that you love and actually matter.

A lifestyle trend to combat the consumerist society and improve mindful living is minimalism, which became prominent in recent years. Minimalism is a practice where people live with as little as they can. Ideally, they live with only what they need to survive and nothing else. This way, they are not holding onto anything in their lives that is not truly adding value to their lives on a regular basis. For the most part, the minimalist trend that you see on various blogs and documentaries are fairly extreme, as they portray individuals with nothing more than a bed, one chair, and one dish for every meal, or something else that is more extreme. You certainly do not have to declutter your life to this extend to feel happy, but it is important to ensure mindfully that everything in your life has a meaning that brings you joy or value in one way or another.

When it comes to decluttering your lifemindfully, there are three areas that you want to look at—your environment, your time, and the people you surround yourself with. You want to make sure that you properly declutter all three areas of your life so that you are no longer holding onto anything that is not adding to the quality of your life. In the following pages, we are going to explore how you can mindfully declutter your life in these three areas in the most effective way possible.

Mindfully Decluttering Your Environment

The area that people most commonly think of when it comes to decluttering anything is their environment. If your environment contains items that you do not need to have, or if you are spending a large amount of time in places that are not helping you enjoy your life, you need to declutter your environment. If you feel that you are not genuinely gaining value from the time that you spend in these areas, you need to let go of them.

When it comes to mindful decluttering, you should always start with the environment that you can physically change. This often includes your home, your car, and your workspace. As you go about mindfully decluttering each of these spaces, you want to make sure that you create the experience in a way that allows you to be mindful the entire time. This means that you should mindfully set aside time where you can address each area of your home, car, and workspace. Set aside as much time as you need in order to achieve a cleaner space. As you go about cleaning your space, make sure that you are present in the moment and that you are honestly considering each element of the space that you are decluttering. Anything that does not bring you joy, add value to your life, or help you live a higher quality of life should be given away or thrown away depending on what it is. Mindfulness is crucial here, as mindfulness will help you honestly determine whether or not you truly want to keep something in your life. If you are truly mindful, you will know that you do not need to keep something just because it was special to you at one time or because it was special to someone else. Instead, you know that anything that does not genuinely add meaning to your life now can be released and can move on to its next home.

Always make sure that as you go through decluttering, you truly pay attention to what matters in your life. It can be easy to get swept away in feeling obligated to keep things or thinking that something has value when it truly doesn't. Remember that just because you paid money for something, it does not mean that you have to keep that item, especially when you realize that it is not something important. You are allowed to change your mind or decide that you no longer want or need that item in your life, allowing you to let go of that item for someone else to enjoy. It is not wrong for you to decide that you no longer want to keep something unless it truly matters to you to keep it.

After you have addressed your physical clutter, there is one more element of your environment that you need to address. You also need to be mindful of the places when you are spending your time regularly, including the restaurants you eat at, the stores that you love visiting, houses of your loved ones, and any other physical venue where you spend your time. While you may not be able to change what these venues look like, you can control whether or not you spend any time in them. Honestly consider whether or not you enjoy spending time in these places, and, if you realize that you do not, begin searching for a new place to spend your time. Spending time in places that are overwhelming, uncomfortable, or unenjoyable solely out of habit is something that many people do, yet it makes no sense. Instead, you want to make sure that wherever you spend your time should be a place that provides comfort, joy, and meaning to you. Otherwise, you need to let go of these places and pick new ones.

When you are planning to go out with loved ones or spend time anywhere outside of your home, pause to consider the venue. Are you going to be comfortable there? Do you enjoy spending time there? Will there be any unnecessary stressors that could make the event uncomfortable for you? Be honest in identifying your needs, especially when it comes to enjoying yourself, and do your best to spend more time in places that are comfortable and which create an enjoyable experience. Avoid places that make you feel stressed when you are supposed to be enjoying and relaxing. This way, you can fully immerse into the experience of enjoying yourself and the company that you keep, rather than spending your time trying to make up for the stress that this place brings.

Mindfully Decluttering Your Schedule

Your schedule is another area of your life that you need to declutter. In today's age, we wield the word "busy" with pride, as if never having time to slow down and enjoy life or take care of ourselves is somehow a negative thing. This likely stems from the fact that we like to attempt to justify why we are overexerting ourselves, even when it is less than ideal, and an alternative option should be chosen.

Decluttering your schedule is something that should be done on a regular basis to ensure that you are not accumulating more than you can handle in your everyday life. You should also keep a decluttered schedule in mind whenever your boss, for example, asks if you want to add something else to your schedule. This ensures that you are not overextending yourself or stretching yourself too thin just to please other people. Learning how to fill your schedule mindfully and in a way that brings you joy and serves you is important, as this ensures that every aspect of your schedule is worth the energy that you spend.

When you create a new schedule, make sure that you honestly account for everything for that needs to go on your schedule and to-do list. This means that your work, obligations, hobbies, your downtime, and even your bedtime should all be mindfully considered and organized into your schedule so that you are engaging in a day to day experience that serves your well-being. When you mindfully build your schedule in a way that accounts for your needs, obligations, and desires, you ensure that you are leaving plenty of time for everything to get done. This way, not only are you meeting your obligations, but you are also meeting your needs and leaving time for you to enjoy your life, too. All of these aspects of your schedule are important and need to be adequately accounted for so that you can create a schedule that truly brings joy and value to your life.

When you begin to address your schedule, it may be challenging for you at first because you find yourself engaging in old habits around scheduling. You may find it to be challenging to account for your needs, to create enough time for entertainment, or to refrain from willingly giving up your needs in order to fulfill someone else's needs. All of these are habits that are frequently picked up by people in our society, and this can lead to increased stress and an overwhelming schedule.

A great way to declutter your schedule and keep it that way is to begin exercising strong boundaries when it comes to how you spend your time and what you are willing to invest your time in. Do not be afraid to learn how to say "no" to people who request more of your time than you can reasonably offer. In doing so, you ensure that you are protecting the time that you need to use to keep yourself healthy and happy. If you do find that you have extra time in your schedule that can be used to help someone else or add something else into your schedule, ask yourself if you honestly wish to add this new activity into your schedule. If you feel that adding this new activity to your schedule would bring value or joy into your life, then you can certainly do so. If not, mindfully accept that this is not something that you wish to do, and you should decline the offer. This way, you continue to respect and protect your time and uphold the boundaries that prevent your schedule from becoming decluttered with unwanted activities.

Mindfully Decluttering Your Social Circle

In the age of social media, it can be easy to collect people into your social circle who do not truly need to be there. At one time, social media was intended to be used for us to keep up with the people whom we know, but these days, it seems to be used for much more than just that. These days, people add friends and follow every person they meet, as well as countless people whom they have never met. They keep these people in their social networks as a way to stay in touch with them. While some of these people may actually be your friends, in many cases, some of these are people who you do not enjoy talking to or having a connection with. In addition, they may be people whom you like a lot, but you tend to compare yourself to them, causing you to feel as though you are "less" and unworthy.

Beyond social media, we also tend to do this with our everyday lives, even in person. We keep people around out of obligation rather than desire, as we fear that if we were to remove someone from our lives, we would be seen as cruel or mean in some way. We do not want to hurt anyone's feelings or create any form of conflict in our lives, and so instead of letting people go from our lives, we continue to keep them around and engage with them even though we do not benefit from the connection.

I'm not saying that everyone in your social circle does not need to be there, but there is a good chance that you are keeping more people around than you need to. Decluttering your social circle can be a healthy way for you to let go of some people who have been taking up space in your life and causing stress or discomfort in any way so that you can have more time for yourself and the people whom you truly enjoy spending time with.

A great place to begin your mindful decluttering of your social circle is directly on social media. Go through your friends list and the list of people you follow. Start weeding out anyone whom you do not truly enjoy engaging with. If you come across someone on your feed, for instance, and you feel rolling your eyes at this person, then you should be deleting that person from your list. Likewise, if you find yourself judging that person or only following them so that you can feel better about yourself and your life, then you should delete that person from your social media account. Removing people whom you do not genuinely connect with and those who do not encourage you to feel better about life in a positive and healthy way is going to clear up your social media pages and make it easier for you to design a social media experience that is more enjoyable. You will realize that as you scroll your new and decluttered feed, you feel significantly better because you are not constantly growing annoyed by the unwanted posts showing up on your newsfeed.

After you have sorted through your social media, you also need to sort through the people in your actual life. When it comes to mindfully decluttering your social circle, it can feel challenging to know how to do it. You might feel like releasing someone from your life requires some form of formal goodbye, where you let them know that you are not spending time with them anymore and that you are moving on with your life. While certain relationships may require a conversation like this, most will not, as they are likely the kind of people, who do not need this level of goodbye from you. The chances are they are just acquaintances or people whom you barely know and can easily be released from your life simply by choosing not to engage with them any longer. As you remove them from your social media and choose to stop spending time with them, you will find that they naturally fall away from your life without any need for confrontation or significant conversation regarding the ending of your relationship. In fact, for many of these people, they may be feeling the same way about you, which makes it even easier to let go of them from your life when the time is right.

For more personal relationships where you have been closer with the individual, it can be quite challenging to decide how you are going to close out your relationships. For many people, we are not taught how to respectfully and tactfully end relationships in a mindful way that allows us to respect the other person while respecting ourselves, too. Without any clear understanding of how you can end relationships in a peaceful and polite manner, it can feel as if you are being tasked with the most challenging thing in the world, which may be the reason that you continue to maintain this relationship, even though you are ready to end it. In this case, learning how to end more significant relationships with people whom you no longer wish to share a connection with is important.

When it comes to ending relationships that are more significant, there are several steps that you can take to end it in a way that will be more peaceful and less painful for everyone involved. Understand that mindfully decluttering your social circle by ending relationships that you no longer wish to maintain can be more challenging than any other form of mindful decluttering. In these scenarios, you are not just giving away an old pair of shoes or choosing to hangout in a new location. Instead, you are choosing to end a relationship that has been significant and meaningful for you in the past, making it much harder. There are two people involved, and both people have feelings that stand to be hurt in this experience. Ending the relationship properly is important to ensure that it goes as smoothly as it possibly can.

As you end a relationship with someone, whether that is a friendship, a close family relationship, or a romantic relationship, you need to make sure that you commit to honesty and transparency with why you are doing it. You do not want to lie about the reason that you are ending a relationship, as this can lead to an even more uncomfortable and hurtful situation. While you are being honest and transparent, make sure that you are doing so in a way that is polite and considerate. You do not want to end a relationship with rudeness, as this can lead to you to create unnecessary animosity and emotions, which may also lead to an intense amount of guilt and shame later on. Remember, at one time, this person meant a lot to you, and you were very close, so you need to respect that by being gentle and polite.

After you have a difficult conversation with the individual, you need to commit to keeping the relationship ended. When a relationship has ended, it can be easy for you to start feeling guilty and to feel as though you have to apologize and make up for it and go right back to being in a relationship with the person whom you want to leave behind. Trust that this is just a part of the process of grieving the end of a relationship. You have to allow yourself to feel guilty and in denial. As you work through them, you will eventually find yourself feeling at peace with the situation and having closure from the ending of the relationship. Then, you will be able to grow forward and welcome new and more beneficial relationships into your life.

Chapter 9

Continuing Your Mindful

Growth Journey

If you want to develop a mindful life and awaken to your best self, it is important to understand that you are going to be embarking on a lifelong journey, not a one-time fix up that only lasts for a short period. Just because you have come this far in addressing various areas of your life with a mindful approach, it does not mean that yourjourney is suddenly over. Instead, it simply means that you have effectively begun to lay the foundation for a strong, mindful future that is more aligned with what you desire to experience in your life. If you want to continue to find joy in all the benefits of living a mindful life, you need to educate yourself on how you can continue to live mindfully moving forward.

Until now, you have been guided and directed on how and when you should be engaging with mindfulness. You have been shown the very habits that you need to address, the behaviors that you need to change, and the strategies that you need to put into place in order to live a mindful and awakened existence. Now, you need to learn about how you can identify when a situation calls for mindfulness, how mindfulness can be applied, and what you can do to live your best mindful life possible. In a sense, this is how you are going to take the leap on your own so that you can really live as freely as possible in your mindful life.

It is important that you take the time to develop these skills in your life, as not knowing how to be mindful on your own can lead you to struggle in living a mindful and awakened life. Each of our lives is so drastically different and unique that we are taken on wonderful journeys that are wildly different from the journeys that other people have. If you truly want to be more of anything in your life, you need to learn the important elements of the skill itself and not just how to apply it to specific situations. This way, when you find yourself engaging in a unique situation that you have yet to read about, you can still identify how you can apply that particular skill to that unique situation.

The steps that you are about to learn are going to take you from doing a mindful edit of your life to becoming a mindful master creator of your own life. You are truly going to awaken to your power now and find ways to begin changing your entire experience through your own personal understanding of what mindfulness is, how it works for you, and how you can personally apply it to various situations in your life.

First and Foremost, Get to Know Yourself

If you truly want to master mindfulness in your own life, you need to put effort into getting to know yourself. At the end of the day, if you do not know yourself, you are going to struggle in making mindful decisions regarding your life because you will not know which decision would serve you best. Living your life based on what other people say is only going to result in you living a life that someone else should be living and not your own life. You will end up doing everything based on what your Mom, friend, boss, or cousin would do, rather than what you would personally do. Take time to explore yourself in every way and watch how this changes your life and support you in becoming more mindful. Spend time alone, try new hobbies, listen to different music, watch various documentaries and educational series, read books, and explore new information so that you can get to know yourself even more. This way, as you continue to grow, you will find yourself having an even deeper sense of understanding around who you are and what you can do to honor yourself in every way in your lifetime.

Pay Attention to Your Needs

As you do get to know yourself, get to know what your needs are, as well as what your desires are. A terrible tragedy that most people fall victim to is not knowing what they truly need or believing that their needs are actually mere desires and that they do not have to get those needs met. In the end, they find themselves feeling as though they are rundown afterthoughts of life because they have not honored their own needs.

A great way to get to know more of what you need in life is to ask yourselfsimply, "What do I need to feel my best right now?" Be honest with yourself, and do not be afraid to say what you truly need. I can guarantee you that your needs are not too much or too excessive, no matter what you believe. Once you have identified your needs, put effort into addressing them by doing what you need. This may mean adding more time to your schedule for self-care, standing up to someone who has been treating you badly, creating boundaries for yourself, or doing many other things that will help you satisfy your needs. No matter what they might be, you want to make sure that you are effectively understanding and meeting your needs to the best of your ability.

Anticipate How You Will Feel, Think, and Perceive Life

As you begin to get to know yourself, you will find that it becomes easier for you to anticipate how you are going to feel, think, or perceive something in various different situations, including ones that you have never been in before. Playing around with theoretical thinking is a great opportunity to explore yourself more while also anticipating how you would handle various situations that you might face in your life. The key here is not to assume that you would actually act this way or that you would ever get into these situations in your lifetime. Instead, it is to explore what you might do if you were in these situations.

The more that you can anticipate yourself and your possible reaction to various experiences that you might have, the more you are going to be able to make decisions for yourself mindfully. This way, you will be

146

able to reasonably factor yourself in and consider how you might feel or behave in either scenario, allowing you to choose the one that is going to be most suited to you.

Learn to Make Decisions That Serve You

The more that you get to know yourself and anticipate your own needs, the more that you are going to be able to make powerful decisions that can genuinely help you experience a better life. Anticipating your own needs or desires is an important part of knowing how to make decisions for yourself, but much more goes into this beyond just anticipating how you are going to feel when it comes to making a decision, one way or another. Learning how to make decisions for yourself mindfully is a skill that everyone should have, and having it for yourself in your life will truly help take you from a mindful person to a masterful mindful person.

There are three crucial steps when it comes to making decisions for yourself. First, you need to know what your goal is in any decision that you are going to be making for yourself. Knowing exactly what it is that you

147

are trying to achieve is going to help you determine the path that will help you achieve that goal. Then, you need to know how to factor yourself into the goal by deciding which path is going to be most helpful to you while also helping you reach your goal. Finally, you need to know how to review the decisions that you have made to determine whether or not they actually helped you get to where you wanted to go. Slowing down to review your own decision-making process and the result of that decision is crucial in helping you discover more about yourself. This also helps you become more mindful of future decision-making experiences.

Begin Doing Things That Matter to You

One of the most wonderful things about being alive in the modern world is having access to so many choices in your life. Being able to make choices for yourself and having options for how you can live your life means that you can create the life of your dreams through your choices. As you face each choice in your life, even if they are as simple as what you want to eat for lunch, make sure that you make choices that matter to you. Choose the things that you like, as well asthose that bring you joy and make your life more meaningful. This way, as you go through your life, you feel happy with the choices that you make, and you feel grateful for the life that you create. Through this, you will find that life only continues to get better and better as you go.

Conclusion

Mindfully awakening to a life that you have created just for you is a process that many people will not experience, largely because they do not even know that this is a possibility for them in their lives. You, however, know better.

You know that there is a life of meaning, purpose, and joy out there for you, and you want to tap into that experience and live your best life. You want to feel confident, empowered, and positive in your life, and you want to know that everything you desire truly is available for you in your life. That is why you have chosen to take the bold steps toward mindfully awakening to the best life that you can possibly have. Your desire to experience a life filled with greatness, meaning, and purpose is so strong that you know that in taking these steps forward, you will unlock a level of satisfaction and joy, unlike anything that you have ever experienced before. You know that for you, this is just the beginning of what might be the best journey of your entire life.

I hope that in reading *Mindfulness, Guide To Awakening*, you have learned about how you can mindfully awaken to your best life, improve your self-esteem and self-confidence, and take meaningful steps toward personal growth and development. By learning how you can lay the strong foundation for a mindful life, all the way to how you can carry on mastering the art of mindfulness in your everyday life, I hope that you have gained everything that you need from this book.

As you continue to grow and develop in life, it is important that you always seek to engage in a mindful manner. Continue to take the time to get to know yourself, to understand yourself, and to have a deep sense of compassion and love for yourself. Respect your needs and desires, and teach yourself how you can be your own best friend by being readily available for yourself as much as possible. Learn how to meet your own needs, consider your desires, and design a life that you love so much that each day when you wake up, you

154

feel confident that you are living your best possible life. Through this, you will also have one of the most meaningful and satisfying relationships with yourself.

When you finish reading this book, I encourage you to spend plenty of time deeply contemplating how you can integrate the tools and techniques discussed in this book. Educate yourself on what it means to be mindful. Place your full focus and awareness on drawing more mindfulness into your life, and be considerate on how you can really use these techniques in your everyday life. The more that you can mindfully integrate these techniques into your life, from having a daily meditation routine to having your own way of boosting your self-esteem or making decisions, the better the outcome of this practice will be.

Remember, mindfulness is a journey that lasts a lifetime, not a one-time edit that is going to change your life forever. Although the steps you have taken here will certainly set the course for life-changing experiences, they are not where your mindfulness journey ought to end. Instead, make an effort to continue being mindful every single day by learning what mindfulness is and how it feels to practice it and then actively applying it to your everyday life. When you commit to living your best life through mindfulness, you will find that it grows easier and that you do not have to put quite so much effort into constantly remembering to be mindful. Instead, it will come naturally to you, and you will be the most mindful person that you can possibly be. Moreover, you will find that the more you practice mindfulness, the more benefits you stand to gain, and the more these benefits will impact your life deeply. It is well worth it to stay committed to these mindfulness practices and grow with them for as long as possible.

Lastly, if you enjoyed reading this book and felt that it supported you in improving your mindfulness in your life while also assisting you with awakening to better life experiences, I encourage you to leave a review on Amazon Kindle. Your honest feedback would be greatly appreciated.

Thank you, and best of luck in stepping into your own mindfully awakened life.